Eden Valley – into the Threshold Light

Introduction

These poems, alongside photographs and paintings by my friend Nick Jones, have been written over a number of years whilst living in and exploring the Eden Valley. Taken together, they offer a meditation upon the people who have settled over millennia and left their memorials in cairns, henges, standing stones, hogbacks, settlements, churches, castles, railways and bridges. They celebrate, as well, the wildlife, trees and flowers, which grow alongside the valleys and waterways of Eden.

The poems are arranged so they start at the springs of Eden and gradually make their way downriver, taking excursions to interesting sights and monuments, to the eventual outflow into the Solway.
Some powerful figures are considered during the journey, such as Lady Anne Clifford and Sarah Losh with their impressive artistic and architectural achievements but also more humble figures who made their mark in different ways.
The patterning and patina of light ever changes in the lea of the Cumbrian Mountains, scattered by shafts of cloud-dappled sunlight, a field suddenly illuminated like a painted Lindisfarne script. The richest light is in the early morning and at dusk, aided in the late spring by the gloam of bluebells beneath river woods, the flush of snowdrops brightening a dark winter morning or the rich tapestry of autumn leaves and bracken.
A mantling of snow transforms the familiar into the rich and strange, offering a further dimension to which I allude in these poems, the 'threshold light' that is present along the Eden itself - a light that at times takes the onlooker beyond the liminal world of eye and ear towards a glimpse of the numinous.
I hope the reader will be able to travel with me along the banks of the river and its people and share some of my imaginings, as well as prompt his or her own thoughts upon this beguiling landscape and its settlers. In all seasons and weathers it has the capacity to take the quiet observer through the doors of perception.

Source

Look down from the threshold of Hell Gill Force,
beneath Wild Boar Fell and Mallerstang Edge;
the desolate moorland left behind,
luminous Eden penetrates deep
between sheer thighs of the valley.

The light is long as evening
deepens the rich green of meadows,
cloud in the distance mutters rain;
drop by drop the young river quickens
as becks churn down valley sides,
evaporation begins its long withdrawals.

Resurgent Eden sucks away at soil,
sublimates in turn, swollen by Scandal,
Helm and Belah, runs towards Kirkby Stephen,
bubbles oxygen as it prattles
under bridge and overarching viaduct.

After Nunnery gorge and Wetheral
it slows, snakes towards Carlisle
and Solway, uncoiling out to sea
a threshold silence, as saturation
dissolves to endless channels,
up and down again.

Eden Springs

A late January sun telegraphs from Hugh Seat, dots
of high ridge cairns stark against the snow line;
Eden springs stutter and bell clear air carries
the gargle of a hundred rivulets dripping
and splashing into Hell Gill, percolating
through limestone into subterranean
channels, gorging and clattering,
forcing a chasm
twenty dank
feet deep
beneath
Hell Gill
bridge.

Rumbustious, rollicking, peat rich water
sluicing through limestone slabs
and pavement, scouring cliffs
and swallow holes down
to the sudden shock
of the falls - slow
motion scatter
over the lip;
seedburst
rockpool
patterns
thump
down
pour
print.

Eden Valley - the Overview

This plenteous Eden brims with sweet water,
invaders love her fertile banks and woods;
she offers questing hearts boundless answer,
the hope of settlement and worldly goods,
the light footfall of each past earthly dancer.

And more, she offers hope and dream,
in spite of ruin and disaster,
Beaker, Carvetii, Roman, Saxon stream
over the hill, breed beasts - each advancer
bright with belief, their wild brains teem.

We make our Eden, thinking makes it so:
clear woods, plant crops, make ceremony,
build walls and towers, ringworks, know
ourselves by circled stones, broken tumuli:
against our anger let the Helm wind blow.

This Eden starts with mountain springs,
gathers force, slakes thirst of beast and drover,
churns monumental skies through rainbow rings
past village green, common, old enclosure,
past longhouse, Pele and standing stones:

sluice through our fears, burst the floodgates of the heart.

The lovers bridged, Hell Gill

A gulphy stream
and tanglewood
on either side
of all that's good;

our hands are stretched
to bridge the gap,
we almost touch
a rising sap;

fingertips
just inched apart,
moistened lips
and beating heart;

to span the space
we need an arch
to bear our weight
and steal a march;

the ceiling sky,
the winter snow,
the sapling ash
of love will grow

and span the space,
the cleft below
and then we'll meet
and then we'll know.

Dent Station, 1,150 feet

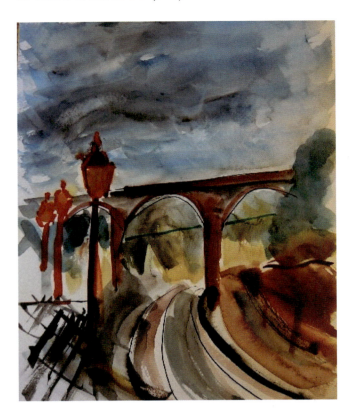

A high road viaducts across declining sky,
rails curve underneath towards dark hills,
dull pewter tracks into gloom.

Station lamps gleam as dusk deepens,
islanded pools of light hemmed by miles of moorland;
a channelled beck murmurs to the east.

November chill clenches Victorian ironwork,
platforms recede into silence,
honeycombed hills lean in, tunnel mouths yawn.

A tawny owl calls across the valley,
gusts of wind scratch brittle leaves across clinker,
distant village lights wobble and flicker.

Agitated rain and wind against drystone walls,
sheep cough into the stretched ear of night,
faint rumours sigh along exposed rails.

The traveller breathes in, watches, listens:
feeble lights, murmuring shadows of hills;
cloud-concealed stars break through, held breath released.

Garsdale Station

Out of Kirkby Stephen, hills smudged by showers,
rails grind on and on and round the bend,
the black hole of Birkett tunnel and sudden light
out onto Ais Gill summit - blurry rain,
a suggestion of sheep, Shotlock hill and
Moorcock tunnels - shoot through loud and dim,
empty moors, Dandry Mire viaduct -
two hundred and twenty seven yards -
Garsdale next – in the distance a blur
of station buildings, four lamps, white weatherboards
snake behind a single spruce, red signal down,
slow down, drop a single traveller
in the deserted station,
watch him fade into distance.

Lady Anne Clifford – Thole and Think On

Lady Anne breasts the steep rise from Skipton,
reins horse and stares down from Hell Gill:
the Old Highway falls to Thrang where Eden,
far below, streams over limestone shelf, still
stirred by Hell Gill Force, tight, battered, swollen.

First the chapel at Outhgill, then castle ruin
as far as eyes can see - her own Pendragon -
Lammerside, Wharton, Hartley, far Castle Hewen
beyond her Brough, Appleby and Brougham:
a force bubbles through her mind, a fusion.

Her Eden will be restored, castles, churches,
family fame made new - she has the power,
for years has faced down dominant rivals
contesting titles and estates, who would sour
her will and pride, mouth firmed by such survivals.

Sixty now, she recalls herself dressed as Berenice,
the costume by Inigo Jones, that Whitehall Masque
long ago, the court, a young girl firmly bodiced,
'much beloved by that renowned Queen Elizabeth...'
She wears plain black now, the river is her voice.

St Mary's churchyard, Mallerstang

1870-1875
'In memory of those men and their families who died
during the construction of the Settle-Carlisle Railway and are buried
in the churchyard. Erected in 1997 by Public Subscription.'

Look left as you walk in, a sandstone
rock with brass plaque records the deaths
of labourers and their families;
within a semi circle of small stones
clusters of red and yellow pansies
splash colour amidst grass and graves.

Malnourished and broken bones lie
beneath twenty five unmarked graves
alongside vicars and villagers,
before and since, who left their mortal coil,
looked over by Caedmon, monk of Whitby,
and other northern saints in stained glass.

Lady Anne Clifford 'newe repayred' this church
in sixteen sixty three, the porch inscription boasts;
two centuries later what would she have made
of railway sleepers here and parallel
lines less than half a mile across the river
glimpsed beyond collapsed and cold Pendragon?

Let's say she wraps her woollen cloak more close,
stares down her much beloved valley
and, speaking for bereft women,
offers her almshouse in Appleby
and of the ruins and the dead declaims:
'Know heaven and fame contaynes the best of them.'

Pendragon Castle
'Let Uther Pendragon do what he can,
Eden will run where Eden ran'

A deep crescentic ditch,
crossed by two causeways
protects the Norman Keep,
whose massive walls,
four metres thick,
honeycombed with vaulted chambers,
still partly stand,
a skeletal framework
about a collapsed centre
it could not hold.

Defiant stones still rear
above a skittish Eden,
where legend has it Uther
Pendragon tried to channel
the river through his moat,
thwarted by two dragons,
controlled by Merlin.

Burnt twice by Scots and twice rebuilt,
last by Lady Anne in sixteen sixty:
'The restorer of the breach,
The restorer of paths to dwell in,'
sketched by Buck and Pennant,
still standing, in the eighteenth century.
The corner turret or garderobe tower
with latrines on the two upper stories
withholds its secrets.

Pendragon in the distance,
Wild Boar Fell to the south,
the Eden still breathless from Hell Gill,
on the Old Highway from Wensleydale
Lady Anne looked down on her ruin:
'...age has left nothing but the name
and a heap of great stones...'

Oak Tree, Wharton Hall

Behind this necromantic oak lies
Wharton's fortified ruin,
14th century, H-shaped,
crumbling gatehouse, solar tower,
vanished banquet hall.

Centuries of sheep, sodden rot of rain,
have made a hollow cave of heartwood,
where ticking years, siege and swords
passed by, lopping branch, stringing
felons, foes and favourites gone cold.

Still, each spring, buds burst, birds nest
and walkers stop to stare and guess
at stories spliced by arrow heads
and nails and lovers, casting all their skins
to find a shape more svelte to bask in.

Lady Anne Clifford Brough Castle 1665

Clifford Tower, the windowseat,
December, a damp, raw day,
restoration is complete,
my mother would be content.
Brough, Brougham, Skipton, Barden,
all our castles repaired,
Appleby, Pendragon,
it is finished – chapels, churches,
I have left my mark, unbidden.

This round tower, four centuries since,
Robert Clifford constructed,
and here I sit and convince
myself all will be well,
roofs, gates, turrets, garderobes
maintained when I am gone.

I see the church from my window,
where my steward, Gabriel Vincent,
'chief director of all my building,'
lies buried. He died in the Roman
Tower, as I call it, built from stones
from the Roman fort Verteris,
'The Summit' – and so I sit, deep
in thought, so many battles won,
so many people lost, old stones
brought down, reused, dislodged again.
The Cliffords may pass, the estates
and titles lost, the castles ruined…

I have recorded all that I have done.

The Loki Stone, Kirkby Stephen

Sharp jawed, triangular head and beard,
ram's horn ears, twist pained mouth, bound arms, trapped
above the wrist, his hands caught and hanging limp,
legs stocked and chained, feet forced to the right,
creative energy downcast, crestfallen.

Loki, the shape shifter curtailed, his mischief-
making mocked, imagination sheathed;
the foster brother of Norse God Odin,
his nether half, like Milton's Satan,
full of guile, suggestion, envy-pricked.

But look, his head, though sliced above the temple,
trepanned by the edge of stone, is joined
again along the top, as if the carver
felt the spirit had measures more,
not to be confined to vertical space.

The Viking demi god in stone, Loki,
the Joker and inventor, irritator
of the orthodox, magician, song maker
on the other side, chained but branching
out in uncontainable thought.

The artist, like carvers of misericords,
recognised, perhaps, a censored spirit.
They hid their oak Green men, beasts and breasts
beneath a slab for slumped bottoms, he wrapped
his point of view over the top, just out of sight.

Loki - Fire god

You'll find me
at your most elemental,
the overwhelming urge
to plunge deeper, darker,
down the hot abyss.

You'll find me
in the sharp plummet of flight,
the falcon-steepled dive,
a salmon thrust
against the fall.

You'll find me
in the spurts of flame
within a driftwood fire,
warm against the evening dark,
the hiss of waves.

I'm there
in the red poppy's swirl of skirts,
its black lace, tented mogul tower,
the narcotic scent,
deep centred;

when you wake up
ready to run and dance,
ride and sing,
ready to take on the world
and win.

Loki at the Threshold

They found him at the threshold -
changed to a salmon,
he'd tried to leap the net
but Thor grabbed him,
wrapped him in a copy
of his invented net,
carried him back to Asgard.

Bound between three rocks
with the sinews of his son,
poison dripped onto his face
with Sigyn his wife watching;
she tried to catch the poison
but each time she emptied a cup
poison needled his face again.

His convulsions were earthquakes
and they laughed – he should endure
until Ragnorok, the end of the world.
Fools to think he would submit,
the revenged gods left him
to focus on conquest
- their will to be done.

Each day Sigyn empties the cup,
each day it fills again;
both know it will not end
till greed and suspicion
but cast more nets to catch
a wiser way, study fish, fowl, tree and sky,
the dreams of a bound chrysalis
for the fictive, captivating butterfly.

Boundless Loki

He struggles, learns,
rescales his lore;
manacle burns
imprint a score,
a smile remains,
the bonds are loosed:
like paper chains
his brain's unsluiced.

St Andrew's, Crosby Garrett

"Arklow, 'hill of sacrifice', place
of defence, of heathen worship;
then mission station, wooden cross
for preaching, on top of the hill;
next, a defended dwelling place,
with an oratory through a tall,
Saxon, narrow door to the east.

The Norman rebuild, with three bay aisle,
my watching face on the east capital
of the arcade, whose curled beard and cap,
bespeak pride; my donor commissioned,
the same masons who built Lowther
to carve me and a squint to the North Aisle.

A new chancel in the fourteenth
century – Priest Sandford left twenty
shillings for a new bell, still used.

Arklow hill, elevated, tranced;
oracle above the village,
viaduct and distant fells,
my capital face crumbles,
old stones, green with damp, soften
into sand, countless hymns seep
from walls like heartbeats winding down,
the faithful dwindle, their prayers faint,
St Andrew's settles on its knees…

whatever is to come, witness to its taking place."

The Clifford Tombs - St Lawrence, Appleby

'Who Fayth, Love, Mercy, Noble Constancie to God, to Virtue, to Distress, to Right, Observd, Exprest, Shewd....... Know Heaven and Fame Contaynes the Best Of Her.'

Such you described your mother;
much the same could be said of you,
though one could add obstinacy,
a deal of power-defying pride
and courage – neither would suffer
fools, be they husband or king, both
fiercely loyal to those in their care.

A black plinth for your mother's
alabaster figure, exactly
carved by the queen's sculptor, Colt;
hands in vertical prayer, the sun
illuminates soft stone fingers
and feet, the buttons of her dress;
unflinching, she looks heavenwards,
gilt coronet steady, the folds
of her cloak, her steadfast expression
pious, perfectly marbleised.

Your own tomb is severe, unfigured,
though proud of your full, shapely form
and talk, upon which Donne remarked:
'She knew well how to discourse of all things
from predestination to sleeve silk.'
Twenty-four shields show titular pride;
below, your life starkly inscribed: 'Here lyes...
Ye dead body of Lady Anne Clifford....'

Margaret and Anne, uncompromising
to the end - you wrote your epitaph
twenty years before you died, nothing
left to chance, placed beside your mother.
Your tombs and works proclaim the best of you.

Unforeseen

And so to reach the sandstone bridge,
scan the pointing, piers and parapet,
to imagine each foot,
wheel, hoof and pad
plod, turn and tread…

and to lift your eyes,
see two banks joined,
the rising span
with flood-resisting piers
reach across the water
like a stone rainbow…

and somewhere,
on the other side,
the furtherance of a dream.

Warcop Old Bridge

A span of thirty-seven metres,
with three segmental arches
strengthened by four ribs of tooled ashlar;
each side of the bridge
four simple waterspouts
drain surface water;
there are two pairs of refuges,
three-sided,
to protect frail bones
from passing traffic.

You can imagine yoked oxen and wagons,
pack horses, tinkers and soldiers
stumbling over cracked flags
and cobbles, cattle and fowls,
pedlars and mummers clattering
over dust and dung-laden centuries.

Constructed before thirteen forty,
it hunches in stolid sandstone,
two piers over three metres thick,
whose cutwaters knife aside floods
that have crushed each medieval bridge
spanning the Eden but this -
its hippo-like solidity,
squat sandstone legs and barrelled torso
defy all odds.
Warcop - last bridge standing.

To Catch the Bridge at Warcop

I cannot wait to catch
the ancient bridge at Warcop,
to touch the old bridge...

I will stop in the middle,
lean over the worn sandstone
enclosed in a refuge,
look down to the water,
watch it gliding through
the old arches, lift my eyes
upstream, watch and listen.

I will see much in the water:
waving green weed, eels,
stickleback, a few salmon,
the call of birds all around,
mallard alarms, piping
oystercatchers, a grumble
of greylags grazing the fields,
the white sails of swans,
a rising of skylarks
wringing the light of rain,
the long trills of a curlew
dying away in the distance.

The narrow stone bridge
curves right to a flood field,
where a tall man in bobble hat
and blue fleece works intently;
with quick strokes of his pencil
he sketches himself
sketching on the bank
near the ribs of an arch.

I watch him watch the bridge,
narrow his eyes,
and catch it keen
as the centuries edge
of the stone cutwaters.

Tree Cross, Ormside

You stand on step three of five flights of steps,
which fall away from a large sycamore
where the cross should be. Live wood replaces stone,
human weight wears a few more grains of sand.

Behind, two gate piers lead to St James,
squat towered, high up on a ringwork;
a channelled beck chunters nearby and Milly
wags her way towards the church and hall.

Side by side we step forward, pass through
the pillars, pause, look back to the tree cross,
the lane alive with preachers, butter sellers,
millers, masons, lovers, honking geese, dust.

Up towards St James we see earthworks,
soldiery, men of power, palisades,
smoke from burnings, the smack of chisel on stone.
Three tiers of narrow lancets stare from the tower.

An east wind sways branches of the cross,
leaves thrash as it blows up the ringwork, down
to a curve of Eden, where blurred reflections
on the old ford, wobble the viaduct beyond.

Ormside, St James

The approach passes a mediaeval cross,
within living memory site of the butter market,
the cross gone, just a square of tiered steps
falling away from a large sycamore;
below, and south east, squats Ormside Hall,
with its gatepiers, cobbled yard and old barns,
the fourteenth century tower and cross wing,
two windows with trefoil headed lights.

Saxon St James sits on an older earthwork,
its defensive twelfth century tower
with three slender lancets, overlooks Eden,
a beacon for the ancient ford half blocked.
Light penetrates the mullion-shadowed nave,
its tall, early doorway with rough hewn lintel
now serves as a window; a roman altar
is inset into the porch - gravid statements.

A high mound, Romano-British or earlier,
a place of power, a place of worship,
exclusive and enclosed, looking outwards;
of hope and fear, of ours and theirs,
gods and fabulous, intertwined creatures
of the Ormside bowl, their frontal gaze transfixed,
its Anglian silverwork unsurpassed,
looted and buried beside a warrior.

In the chancel wall a leper's squint,
a hagioscope, with an elevated,
'holy' view through to the high altar
for the excluded lepers - their fate
to look in and long for what was not to be:
the Pele tower standing against, the church
with its hierarchies, the silver, glass and gilt bowl,
once unparalleled, reduced to a drinking urn.

Off the rails, Appleby

Russet buffers with black spots,
old impacts forgotten
like a shard of ladybird…

circles and cylinders,
rectangles and funnels,
windows on the curve…

footplate clang of clog,
sweat, shovel and roar,
whistle shunt and steam…

silent rust and winter branch,
lattice bridge and lantern…

cross the line

where carved weatherboards,
pitch pine benches
and gothic gables wait

beside the rails.

Dufton Churchyard – a Ladder Way over the Wall

Coming from many ways
in the wanderings of careful thought:
find a ladder over the churchyard wall,
threshold gained; here is shelter
from the world's gale,
refuge from life's long days
which catch you by the throat,
knowing lungs must fail.

All day on the Old Highway,
a last climb to see wider,
further, deeper than you could imagine…
a place neither yours nor his, nor hers,
breath let go, slowed heartbeat,
measured inhalation, to stretch forth,
take the next step onward, outward, upwards.

Saxon Tympana, Long Marton

A dragon looks back over its shoulder,
its tail in a knot, little black ears alert
to the pricking on its back from a winged
shield with a cross and sword.

Beside, threatening to swamp the boat
it stands in, an ox with elongated neck
and bird's head – is it attempting to fly,
between elements, to flee the earthbound,
one foot poised beyond the gunwales,
such doubtful surety all but left behind?

The beaked bird has spread its wings, looks west
ready for the take off; his pricked and knotted
friend the dragon, spurts an approving streak
of flame in his direction.

All you who approach this threshold,
stand prepared to be translated,
let go your feet of clay,
unfurl your wings and fly.

Battling Knights, All Saints, Bolton

On the North wall, this rare tablet, a gift:
'Lawrence De Vere to the men of Bolton.'

A gift for what – coming to his aid
in battle, a wager lost? The knight
without a banner, the smaller one,
seems to have hit home, his horse's ears
are flattened, the other leans back, lance down,
throat speared - De Vere himself or rival,
whom the men of Bolton unsaddled?

They'll kill and torch, tear down, bludgeon,
so driven to breed, guard, sustain,
they give fealty to power which shields;
do we not ourselves, for the dream
of seeming safety, who stare and judge
centuries hence, at shocking violence?

Nine hundred years pass,
tablets remain, writ large
on the church wall, De Vere
established debt,
community ties,
faith and kin,
ours and theirs,
to tilt again,
complicit.

Holy Dusters, St Lawrence, Morland

Attached to the foot of the Saxon tower,
dimmed by interior midweek glooms,
a notice to those with cleansing power:
Lulu's November, so, she assumes,
Patti and Janet share December's dark hour.

Picture Lulu, strenuous with duster,
the parish chest could do with a polish,
the font with its heavy lid - in a fluster
with the carving of Christ - don't demolish
the reredos with desire for lustre.

Patti comes early and calmly climbs
all twenty two foot of oak tower ladder
and screams in the dark to trenchant chimes
of the morning bell, laughs and cries, sadder,
gladder than for years; how many times

has she pictured that scream? Now it's done,
she can return to earth and temperance.
Janet smiles into the alms dish, no nun,
she buffs the nine male heads with reverence,
an angel, and sighs for her long lost one.

There's Sheila, Carole, Judith, Jean, dear Dot,
who performs twice, as does Ann, bless her;
next week the dust they brush is back to squat,
dust to dust, the memories all blur
in this church they love, thole, and find the plot.

Hand on the Bridge, Temple Sowerby

Who carved the hand?
Perhaps forty years ago warm nerved,
strong fingered hands chiselled
sandstone, impressed lines
on the bridge parapets.

A concentration,
wanting to get it right,
a left statement, your hand
on the bridge, long fingered,
confident, held down quietly.

Cars, lorries
they roared past
forty years ago,
now bypassed,
sidelined.

Still there,
spattered now
with yellow lichen
and black age spots,
your hand, still on the bridge.

Hands on Hearts, Temple Sowerby Bridge

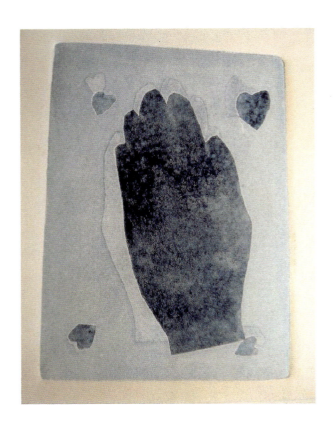

Pale lilac hand
beneath dark blue
left over right
nearly held true

Each corner
a blue heart
half covers
a light heart

Carved on the bridge
a felt thought
cut to the shape
hand heart caught

Mayburgh Henge

Myriad stream smoothed stones
heaped high by blood warmed hands,
those millennial cold bones,
crushed to riverbed sands.

Many gathered round
this stony cranium,
pipes shrilled, voices rebound,
danced to Elysium.

Like a life's scattered thought,
stored in granular cells,
a circumference caught
where immolation dwells.

Venture the contoured cirque,
ash root sifted stones,
hear by wind whipped quirk,
the single cromlech's moans.

The Poor Box, Ninekirks

Near the entrance to St Ninnian's,
a simple box upon a leg of oak;
the slit for coins, conscience worn,
solid iron locks the lid against
a desperate poor – the vicar,
doubtless, dispensed alms as he saw fit.

' REMEMB/ ER THE/ POOR'
carved crudely on three sides,
date stamped with Lady Anne's heavy
hand, her latest restoration;
churches, castles, locks and tombs –
all clearly bare her words and deeds
for all to witness – oak, stone, glass,
paint and shield, ungainsayable.

Four 'Bears', Dacre

Before Athelstan's hapless 'Peace of Dacre',
before Bede and the wooden monastery,
four Beasts stood guard, watched every acre,
for pointy threats to hard won dynasty.

A tickling or tormenting, jumped their backs,
some creature, cat or lion, would not be beaten,
reached for, enfolded, biting off attacks,
held up, accused, summarily eaten.

Pooley Bridge

A calm evening jetty,
washed clean as the sky
in a reflective lake.

There is no ferry,
it left long ago
and steams unheard,
dragging shadows along hills.

We are waiting
for the return,
the boards are scrubbed,
railings gleam in the half light.

We have packed our bags,
said our farewells,
stare into silence.

On the horizon
dark mountains gather cloud;
in the middle distance
slight winds ruffle the surface:
a disturbance approaches.

Is that a smudge of smoke
beneath the cloud,
a gleam of richer light?
Do we imagine it?
Is there a hesitation in the wind,
the pressure of an unseen prow
pushing water forward,
as it arcs towards us?

The Ousby Crusader, St Luke's

This wooden effigy, this knight
with legs crossed, calm, enigmatic
mouth, helmet, mail, and sword,
endured a lively afterlife.

A rare, oak tomb cover, this painted
soldier, seven hundred years ago,
maybe dragged back from the Holy Lands,
as sentry, decoy, statuary,
or catafalque for some forgotten
hero, buried in Byzantium.

A symbol, conflicted and confused
of the first crusades, idealism and greed,
a rabble army roused, peasants, knights spelled
by papal edict, visions, schism on all sides.

Centuries after finding rest,
thrown in a field bog by Puritans;
here he lies, safe now in St Luke's,
though sliced through by plough or zealot.

Perhaps his story speaks louder
now than ever – belief is better
held without sword or guns,
listen to other ways, give grace
without favour, favour without score,
make love with zestful spirit, not war.

Croquet at Little Salkeld Mill

Nick the artist takes careful aim,
the wooden ball must pass through each hoop.
the course followed to the very end.

A miss, a setback, a refocus,
the ball aligned again, the narrow
threshold gained a second time.

The millrace, too, must be controlled:
too much water could damage the wheel,
too little, it will fail to turn.

High up above the mill, Long Meg
marshals her circled daughters, mid
summer sun sets precisely on her head.

Precepts abound in government and games,
machines, the spiritual life;
art can question, redescribe, reach
for other ways of entering.

Let free, like Loki, the forbidden,
we yearn to yell and hoop through,
unconstrained, find fulfilling ends,

loosen into fresh beginnings.

Long Meg and her Daughters

Spirals, cup and ring marks, concentric circles,
carvings half obliterated by centuries,
lichen, weather - sisterhoods of stone,
crouched in a circle, watch the admonitory
finger of Meg, which points to the sky.

Stared at under the old ash her sandstone finger
leans between the breasts of Blencathra;
it's as if, hearts in her mouth, we watch as she gapes,
her spiked tooth beyond shorter stumps of stone,
looking out towards the backbone saddle
of a dragon in the distance.

We can ride the dragon, look down,
like Meg, spectators ab extra, pore
over a locked world encircled with stones,
whose undiscerned astronomy,
sacrifice and ceremonies,
our curious wings circle
and circle again.

Kirkoswald Church

Cross the elongated 's' of Eden Bridge,
head north east through specimen oaks,
see the church of St Oswald crouched beneath a slope,
above which the bell tower stands vigil.

For two centuries bells have tolled
for service, wedding, funeral - years before
likely signalled a Reiver raid, while all fled
for refuge to College Pele or castle.

To the west a medieval moated site,
with large, double-ditched enclosure,
in the centre a low platform, where, perhaps,
stood the old castle burnt by Scots in 1314.

A sacred spring of pure, cold water
lies under the nave, accessed through deep
St Oswald's well on the west wall
by a chained, metal drinking cup.

The chancel arch stands on Norman bases,
a two bay south arcade of round arches,
also Norman, still survives, massive
oak beams remain in the Tudor porch.

At the base of two corbels, worn faces
carved from red sandstone smile wryly towards
ribbed Saxon grave slabs, swords and foliated
crosses battened against the North wall.

Nunnery Rapids

It's a slow build up - the calm
once under Lazonby bridge,
the wide, lazy river and certain firmament
with flat banks and scrub willow,
geese skeining overhead and duck skimming low,
the dipper busy about the stones,
inhabiting both air and water;
now darting white chested upstream,
now plunging underwater,
chasing stickleback like an otter.

Then the river quickens,
the pulse swifter,
creaming over rocks,
a palpable fall
with rapids gorging sandstone,
damp and deciduous
with the rooted memory of trees.

Ullswater and the Mallerstang valley flush
the rain of a thousand becks
breaking over dry banks,
dampness rising black wet through mossed stone;
cataract flumed Croglin, sourced from Black Fell,
streaming into Eden beneath burnt red cliffs,
clasped by precarious oaks, their roots
tapped down to the wild waters below,
where salmon scales surge and deliquesce
in scooped out sandstone hollows.

A canoe, tossed with spray, rides the stoppers,
ferryglides subtle paths of the paddle,
dip and sideslip, crests and eddies,
the Eden carrying all in one rooted direction -
watched by nuns whose souls once leapt and yammered
with the river they watched snake and scintillate
out of sight and firmament.

Tabula Rasa, St Michael's Addingham

Hogback gravestones in the porch,
carved along the top with crisscross thatch:
halls of the dead endstopped
by protective beasts with worn out faces,
washed away with the old Daleraven church
by a bridge-crumbling Eden,
to lie in the river bed for centuries;
each winter flood blurred the carefully chiselled,
tooth and claw blunted, the deeds of the dead
erased grain by grain
from collective memory.

But here they lie restored to dry land
alongside carved stone swords,
geometric patterns, cross shafts,
pews, pulpits and stained glass;
each hewn red sandstone of the lonely church
flakes grain like autumn leaves in the long lane.

Carved Faces near Armathwaite

Five sandstone faces,
twice human size,
flattened ellipses
carved into cliffs
above the river Eden,
upstream from the weir.

Moonfaces,
widecheeked
with authoritative vacancy,
eyes open rimmed,
urgently pursed mouths
forming words.

And when the glare
fades from warmed sandstone
and shadows darken,
a dipper crouches still
for a second;
the wagtail pauses,
the interminable river
sucks at the stone,
dislodging grain by grain
its pressed sedimentaries.

His chisel must have pared
without resistance
this soft red stone,
fashioned the sightless five
a countenance from bald suggestion
and as the hammer fell for the last time,
in gathering silence,
with a thrill of complicity,
the carver saw his work whole,
the fivefold vision
over Eden.

Hidden to all but the restless seeker,
weary with pacing worn paths
with familiar insights,
searching for new masks
to express the uncertain outlook,
six feet above the certainties of water.

Sampson's Cave, Nunnery
Source to sea - canoeing Eamont and Eden

April, snowstorm lashed Brotherswater,
our canoe tossed in spray whipped waters,
clatters down Goldrill to dark Ullswater;
waves curl and smash along its eight mile length;
we ship water, lurch and ferryglide
down to Pooley Bridge, sleep under stars,
with the howl of shed dismantling winds...

next day paddle and portage Eamont,
to riversmeet, turn north, Eden Gorge
towards Nunnery, tippling rapids;
wet, chilled, longed-for Sampson's dry cave;
crawl up a steep bank to the tunnel,
dark, twig littered, we strike fire at the mouth,
tea and tales, hot firelight, warmed limbs stretch long
patterns on the roof; we look out
as dusk falls, shadows behind us,
a flickered stream of pipistrelles
pour into twilight – the liminal worlds
of eye and ear melt down, waves of wings,
water, air merge into dream...

        ... third morning: capsize,
cold shock, downstream shiver to Armathwaite,
past castle, round to Hawkcliff Scar,
Fishgarth, Wetheral salmon trap,
Warwick, the Sands, Beaumont, Rockcliffe.

Solway spreads beyond, the distant Offing
and stored away in our heads, the miles
of water, birds and spray, rock and rapids
- rustling through, the whisper wings of a cave.

Armathwaite Castle

On a medieval quoin stone with original mason's marks
a peacock butterfly spreads its wings in the warm morning sun;
for a few minutes it forgets its bedraggled state, soaked for weeks,
hungry, without a mate, this longed-for warmth now present,
it lies still, this moment on this stone, placed six centuries ago.

The stonemason, too, had paused, well pleased,
this castle wall would be work for weeks beyond winter.
He thought back to his girl, she'd cried with relief
and later pleasure, telling him she was with child,
that knowledge-shifting moment warm again in mind.

And Prince Edward might have loitered,
listening to the river that Autumn morning,
mindful of his father, ill in Lannercost,
the Scots and battle, sighed and watched
the sun's play on rapids and castle stones,
newly chamfered window sills, held his sword,
touched blade, frowned and let it go, pleased
to be at one with soothing sun and water,
sheathed thoughts and sounds and lengthening silence.

** A broadsword with a basket hilt was found in the castle;
on one side of the blade 'Edwardus' was inscribed, on the other 'Prins Anglie'
- perhaps left here when his father Edward 1 lodged in Lannercost Abbey.*

Armathwaite, Christ and St Mary's.

Sun pressed stained glass, intensities of blue,
her robe, the sky, the blue bells of Eden....
Burn Jones' blue Madonna prays,
more like a haloed Venus in rainforest,
the paps of a lost paradise behind her.

Her blue light brightens dusty shadows,
lights up a shady sadness in the nave,
picks out one of the millennium tapestries:
Armathwaite shop and post office stitched by I.D;
midweek Christ and St Mary's, pews unweighted,
organ silent, dust undisturbed by the breath of song.

A clatter from the tunnel above the river,
the Carlisle train shunts air down rail towards
the station on the hill and tension
in a thousand churchyard webs
falters fractionally.

December evening, rafters resound
with Christmas carols as the first frost fingers
clench on yew and sandstone. Warmed words
and music rise through plaster and tile
and startle a blackbird into song -
a tawny owl calls across the river
and an answering voice echoes over
valley and hill and far, far beyond
an evening star pulses red and blue.

Armathwaite Bridge

east of eden

From the bridge look east of Eden, look well...
the bankside lime, oak, ash, alder hedge
the river as it pushes on, curves north
blunging red sandstone, gains pace in the rapids
under Hawkcliff Scar, prattles on
past Wetheral and Warwick to the sea.

Look up beyond the river to Cumrew Fell,
walk east and down to Old Water Bridge,
the Pennines, patrolled by hen harrier,
drain north through Geltsdale towards the border,
west down Croglin in waterfalls via Nunnery to Eden.

Here stormwater shoulders its way to the sea,
channels, rips, tears trees, churns silt, rolls rocks,
splits cliffs, an angry brown broil.

But today it reflects cool cloudscapes, ripples
quietly, dippers on the boulders, wagtails
skim the surface, tranced salmon weave gently.

The leisurely becks of Mallerstang and Ullswater
lace downstream, frot and frick over pebbles,
oxygenating themselves towards Armathwaite,

the hermit's clearing, the tower by the ford,
past sandstone faces, and under the bridge
chuckle words, words, words.

Wring the light
The graveyard, St Mary's, High Hesket

You can look down over fields, a few Scots Pine,
to Tarn Wadling, up left to Castle Hewen
and Aiketgate, where our jumbled cottage,
with its thirteen roof windows, lets the light in.

Flanked by drystone walls, an old bridleway leads
down past ash trees, where another forgotten path
follows high water contours of the drained lake,
round to a ruined boathouse.

This is the place to be buried –
for those days when curlews creel in summer skies
and skylarks wring the light of rain and all is still,
the scent of coconut rises from warmed gorse.

Poet's words mouth in and out of mind,
letters from our alphabet kiss and forget,
and so my thoughts when I am gone
love itself will dream upon.

Autumn Webs

Late autumn sun leans against Castle Hill,
lights up a swath of silk at grass level,
where a million spider webs oscillate
between individual blades, that rear
like steeples through valleys of shimmered mist.

Stare through waves of light, crisscrossed, streaked,
single silver strands, intermeshed, covalent,
a dependency, linking myriads
into a world unguessed, through which
foot, hoof and claw trample regardless.

Each day to begin again, repair the night's
destruction, spinnerets weave and knot, adhere,
commonality spread as far as the eye can see:
the remorseless scission of man, bird or beast
cannot crush the will to connect and carry on.

Castle Hewen, Aiketgate.
'On magicke ground that castle stands'

On Hewen Hill the sun is low,
long shadows leak from tree and stone;
stepping upwards, thole and slow
where wind through broken webs is blown
I trample ground where legends moan.

Romano-British stones lie here,
for Celtic stronghold used again
and drystone wallers, losing fear
of thick foundations built for fame,
imagined Arthur back again.

A Cold War bunker, defunct and damp
looks North to borders where bombs might land.
Intact, the Castle and Cathedral stamp
many-centuried feet for the final stand,
that Euen or Caesarius planned.

Their castle's lost in scattered stones,
defiance loiters in the breeze,
disjunctive hints from hollowed bones,
a badger lifts its head to freeze
at human scent, beneath the trees.

With all this rain the drained Tarn's back,
Arthurian Wadling reappears,
a glimpse of sword from the ancient track,
the mind plays tricks as it is steered
by Hewen, through shadowed hopes and fears.

Family Trees, Castle Hewen

These spindly sprigs whistle to the wind,
leafless now, as December rattles through;
an ice-bright sunrise over Crossfell
reddens the old lane, reaching towards
platinum snow on Saddleback, picked out
against the rub-eyed, waking grey, westwards.

First, near the gate, our silver birch, for
twenty-five years; then Beth's sheltered holly
below, Brian's rowan and sapling oaks
dug from Ma's Patterdale garden; then Will's
alder and Jonty's conker, placed in a row
beside drystone walls of the droving lane.

Many years from now, may they be steadfast,
stunted by the wind but strong - and shelter
for the birds; these words may remember how
a sixty-three year old and his dog
watched in the cold dawn and blessed those trees
and his far flung family – and wished for peace

the day after wise-hearted
Nelson Mandela breathed his last.

December 6th 2013

Winter Run, High Stand.

First icy breath, reluctant feet,
turn right, down to Blackmoss Pool;
sunrise throws long shadows, where,
on a field of winter wheat
parallel legs run across the hill;
cloud blurs the sun, a shadow skids
on ice, scrabbles and is gone; fleet
redwings forage the hedgerow,
falling whistles, scratched warble,
their long migration complete.

Climb towards the wood, look back,
Aiketgate in the green distance
lights up, heart pumps elation.
Leap over bush and branch, track
down to the ice-rimmed pool, retrace.
The cast iron signpost smiles letters,
stamped plain in white and black,
beneath which, daffodils planted
in Autumn have broken through;
shadows settle, stack upon stack.

This hour, this one life,
winter running towards the shortest day,
heartbeat, hot breath, slows.

Murmuration of Starlings

Shapeshifters
twisters of dark light
sinewcrossers
strings of DNA
recoiling
rolling out
endless
scribble

fibres of light
dark optics smoking fugues
remaking shiftlight shapeless and shaped
witcheries of wing ripple overhead
circle swirl ripstop
windmaker
clawclutcher
beak agape beak closed
eyes awake eyes shut
whatever cloudshift suggests

look
a straggler
two
peel off flutter away
vulnerable
starling shoals whirr past
catch haul back the escaped
roll again

dusk draws in
chiaroscuro deepens
flutter of wings less spontaneous
describe smaller circles
a black funnel
opens its throat

downswoop
into trees
its done

Absence of Snow

Tracks of badger, stoat and fox
intermingled on the lane
with hedgerow bird
and winded goose;
the stories of the night before
were plain
and printed on the snow.

But this last year or three
an absence of snow
left untold the ways to go,
patterns of claw and pad
offer no guidance
on the old green lane;
our names and numberless
footsteps falter…

writ, like Keats'
on water, water, water.

Broken

Wake into a virus free, snowbright dawn,
icebound Blencathra sears through the window;
good to step out, to feel no weight of shadows,
envisage starting over in warm spring
with whistling birds, translucent leaves, limelight.

A phone call scatters such thoughts like winter leaves,
here and now returns, each sense engaged
as sleep surrenders old continuums.
Irene's mother has fallen on the curb,
broken her nose, shocked, stitched and bruised. We feed
her home made soup and watch the long tailed tits.

Wake into change and hard perspective,
each pitiless, ice-etched ridge and cornice,
collapsed keystones and barrel vaulting
that yesterday seemed quite indestructible.

The mountain's slipped back behind white cloud,
sharp ridges blunted into oblivion;
and this morning's warming world scuttled
into the extravagant and longed-for.

Cracked light

Crack through the door, a shard of dazzle
in the dappled cave, arrowed light…

I can turn over to sleep, withdraw
wide pupilled eyes from stark lucidities;

but lids leak, cellular breakdown
fissures through brickwork round the brain;

black windings, interstellar space,
always the outside trickles in,

affronts the ordinary eye
with shooting starred alternatives.

Let the parallel light squeeze in,
let it cut you to the careless bone.

Fagus Sylvatica by Eden

Here is form – beech trees begin, green and tranced,
a hundred years pass and we write their reports:
the middle one grew straight and tall, multiple-branched,
its limbs smooth and grey, a few lovers' strokes
are written there but they grow slowly elliptical.
In the shade to the right a modest tree
turns away from an elbowed limb, marsupial
droppings harden, wrens nest in hollowed debris,
water slowly drips. This sapling, torn from rock,
rooted firm, grew sideways, reaching for light.
Heavy force on heartwood - root, branch lock
a torsion knot into every yard of growth; tight
sinews, gale twisted, squeezed, leak sap in sun and storm.
Beechmast muffles the forest floor, pale roots start to form.

Black and White

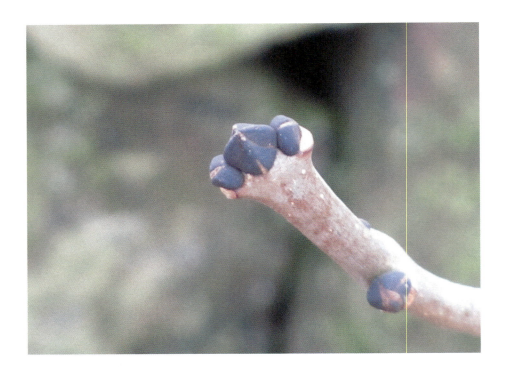

like opinions,
laws,
monochromatic words,
antitheses…

but look!
that black
(or is it the darkest blue?)
ash bud
knuckled frost white,

whose pinnate leaves,
packed green,
(or is it the greenest black?)
quiver for the spring.

Grass a steepled swath of dazzling threads…

December first, low winter sun breaks
through cloud, transfigures a single tree,
bare branches backlit, bright limbs trailing light,
grass a steepled swath of dazzling threads
a moment only and it's gone,
the tree an ordinary, leafless tree
in a field of dull green under leaden skies.

Luminous days drain away,
leave prospects bleak, definition lost -
as torchlit dark, vision shut off,
leaves us stumbling,
blinded by shafts of light.

Hawkcliff Scar

April sunshine east of the river,
sitting under oaks on the hill,
high above the red sandstone
of Hawkcliff Scar.

I watch a curve of rapids
break over rocks
below cliffs of Scots pine, larch
and the nest clattering of jackdaw.

Birdsong and leafbirth stretch
eyes, nose and ears, squeeze out
the clamour of mind,
in a swelling tune of the senses.

My black labrador Milly watches me
as we sit under the tree,
watches now, as I write this,
puts out a paw, touches the keyboard, sighs.

Lying on my back by the river Eden

I lean back on the curved bole
of a beached hazel,
its bark stripped clean,
and stare at the sky,
autumnal pewter and watery blue,
feel the thin warmth of the sun on my face.

I breathe in,
happy for no other reason
than the breath itself,
the fume of river and trees,
balsam and the faint tang
of fox at a distance…

and think that, sometimes,
knowing breath is enough.

Yesterday

The rapids under Hawkcliff Scar,
water that I watched, has scattered
far to Solway Firth.

Sweet breathings of the horse
at Low Holm farm
have vanished into miles of air.

The thoughts composed have wandered too,
twist or turn, today I cannot find
water, breath or thought.

On the Far Bank

On the far bank, bright flowers and trees,
the rapids' fume among the leaves
stirs them gently; a quickening:
bridge me into the same breath.

On the far bank, nuts and berries,
the flash of sun on wings,
a scent of warm resources:
bridge me into the same breath.

On the far bank, voices
whisper over water,
I barely hear the words:
bridge me into the same breath.

On the far bank, solid stones
to build a bridge, to span
the river, taste the airs:
bridge me into the same breath.

Carved names

A quarter century since, we carved
red sandstone on a bluff above
the Eden near to Hawcliff Scar:
Will, Jonty, later Bethan

The clear marks shallower each year,
wind and rain flaking shards away
until they disappeared, wiped clean,
as if the soft stone was never
carved and all our names in vain.

We stamp our feet on earth, make marks
the midnight storm obliterates;
our children start out on tracks,
look back, see dimly, if at all.

Old footpaths on the hills are faint,
but twilight shadows trace lost ways,
broken now by stream and slippage rocks
they straggle on again, high up
till out of sight…

… and so the face, the words I thought
as past, remain. I may not see
or recite them perfectly
but late by evening light
I find the smile you wore when she was born
and first we looked upon our mint fresh child,
and traced the contours of her quickening life.

Otters by Eden

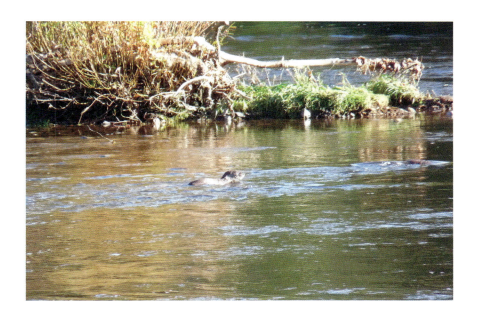

Out of nowhere you're there,
two of you, bigger than I remembered,
gliding in and out of the water,
fur sleeked down,
chasing, gambolling,
tail ferried behind,
now slapped,
now hung
in the air
like a question mark
dissolving
as you dive.

I can hardly believe it
near Low House,
the island,
two of you,
whiskers lit in the autumn sun,
the river smoking with frost
as you snorkel the shallows;
as if life were an endless dive and breath,
breath and dive
today,
now
and nothing else is.

The Garden

Each morning to step very slowly
into lupin light, red swirls of poppy,
see every rosebud more rounded,
outbursts of rosemary blue.

Step by discovering step: how seeded
columbine crane above lady's mantle,
emergent greens jostle and multiply:
all at once flowering, decline, decay.

To weed, unearth the hidden, introduce
fresh plant, take out old wood and blooms,
watch for regrowth and the self sown,
allow the surprise of each day.

Some take instant root, glad eyed
year after year, before fading
to lighten a winter heart, others
spread the strength of their own accord.

The poet's garden holds out its cups
each dawn, closes them at dusk, in cloud;
blurred evening scents intoxicate,
staunch a yearning as the last light drains.

Thrush at Dawn – Feb 2014

After months of rain, drear and dreich,
a dawn decanting from the holly;
focus to a beak unhinged, ajar
with flickered notes, juiced with spring,
a welcome drench to ears and eyes
double-glazed with winter gloom.

Drifts of snowdrop prick pale light
and there you are, chest fluffed, cream noted,
buffeted by wind – branch charmer,
herald of dawn delighting sound,
of brighter days and shorter dark.

Dispel the dirge and dearth,
lance the plug of Winter,
sluice us into Spring!

Toadspawn on Eden

Long strings, double filed
in jellied tubes;

black spotted necklaces
wound among water plants

by sturdy thighs
of the midwifering male,

dark seed nurse
of tacky ontologies;

toadhood in placentachutes
floating towards light.

Spring Gentians

Late spring, in the peaty grass
a scatter of cobalt blue,
shards of Alpine sky fall
to a north Pennine earth.

Late bluebells in Flakebridge Wood
throw a frisson of pale bubbles
beneath dark shaded oak.

Sixty-three springs pass over
and come again, eyebright, tranced.

Feet dance this way, that, blood stirs,
a female blackbird pecks at my feet,
it is a young day, I am a day young,
my old dog rolls on her back and smiles.

A scramble down Cauldron Snout,
waterfalls tumbled and scattered,
a dipper flies to her nest,
gentians open their lids,
breathe in, let go.

Eden Valley Foot and Mouth – Spring 2001

Curlew beaks skirmish
- a distressed screech
of worn metal
spinning
tops

Skylarks falter
in mid flight
listlessly
flutter
back to
earth

choked on the retch and smoulder
of horn and hoof pyres
a flung swallow away
down the lane

Aiketgate

Redstart

A hole in the washhouse wall,
a flash of red, a 'tee-tuc-tuc'
from the apple branch; your silver head,
black cheeks and neck, your Old English
'steort', that firetail quivery,
splayed in a fan of flame winged
tension, beak crammed with bluebottle…

you pass her by on your forage,
her wings a fraction less inflamed
but as urgent and agitated,
as beaks in the nest gape hunger
and instinct drives you blindly on.

Boundaries Soften

Boundary walls soften in snow,

shadows lengthen on castle hill,

footstepped dreams of the way to go,

cold fears slide as the land lies still.

Six Viking Graves, Cumwhitton

Grave I

Her mind reels back to Norseland,
releases a fjord full of memories;
she clasps her maple box, tholes and thinks on …

a key, warmed by her hand, hangs from the brooch
at her breast, oval, double-shelled, gilded;
hot and damp she slides key into lock,
three springs depressed, lid opened, she looks down.

There, her linen-smoother, the glass itself
smoothed by thousands of pressed pleats, strap dresses
held by her brooches, worn over years, worn through
times of plenty and hunger, war and feasts,
the glass pushed and pressed, wrinkles erased…

back to girlhood, dance step by step towards home,
wooded islands and fjords, longhouse stones
warmed by fires, laughter rings, smoke rings, raised horns,
red faces, couplings deep in the forested past.

She can hear her son shouting, a dog whimpers,
her temples pound, she is sweating,
the rain comes down in sheets. What is left?
the buried men sodden in the belly
of their boats, their rusted swords, the burnt oars,
the longship's proud snakehead, burrowed now with worms…

the long sea voyage via Shetland, Orkney,
the sea-shouldering ships, the sickness,
islands - at length the Solway, upstream
towards Hesket and here - slovenly
Saxons with their cross God and afterlife.

Bury me with my gravegoods, my linen,
needles, knife and box – by my head
the single green glass bead he gave me,
who now lies sea-deep, silent, changed.

Sarah Losh 'Re-edifies' St Mary's, Wreay

Taken aback, when he saw Miss Losh's plans,
Bishop Percy thought them 'crude', 'wanting light.'
But Sarah required to be left 'unrestricted
as to the mode of building.' She had her way,
as she often did against powerful men,
who bent their will against hers.

She wears an ironical smile, dresses the part,
but will not be possessed, fierce intelligence
cloaked in muslin and silk. 'Soda maker'
she calls herself, no feminine frills
as gardener, architect, sculptor, mason.
Mistress of many trades, the language of grief
carves through convention, her alabaster voice
transparent, her 'unpolished' style eclectic.

Precise in detail, her fossils and foundry,
quarried stone new made, sisterhood of faiths
lost and found, she chiselled hard won, enduring love.

Pallida Imago – in memoriam Katharine Losh

26th February 1835
It was as if she had lost part of herself,
lost her shadow,
she looked into the mirror,
saw no reflection.

Woodside, the house they shared,
suffused with intimate talk,
whose sun-facing facade
now lay shuttered, dense with silences.
Her clothes, once fashionable silks,
now sombre greys, blacks, mauves.

Katharine's death unleashed all Sarah's languages:
of art, religion, alkali, iron works,
architecture, the unearthed histories,
Roman, Celtic, hammered in her mind.
From alabaster quarried at Wragmire,
she carved fossils, pinecones, lotus flowers,
ears of corn, butterflies – each piece
embellished for Katharine, a rebirthed church,
rich with shared symbolism, old faith, animistic.

Lone years later, she builds a solid catafalque,
anguished, cold, the heavy memory of stones.

In the dark, marble white, Katharine sits barefoot,
ankles crossed, half smiling, a pinecone in the folds
of her dress. Entombed, where sun can scarcely reach,
her spirit flutters in a desolate cell
where Sarah might anatomise her grief.

'For in all things I saw one life.....'
Sarah Losh's alabaster stencils St Mary's Wreay

Thinly sliced, creamy sheets
of soft alabaster,
from Roman mines at Wragmire Moss,
precisely cut, sheathed in glass,
let light play in the Apse.

Stencilled fossils, revealed in mines,
coral leaves and fern,
pattern tracery light,
shapes lost to sun and time
shine through again.

A dim, contemplative light
streams geological strata
to reprise layered symbols
from Egypt, the Orient, Rome, Greece:
One life from many, here as one.

Scan The Light

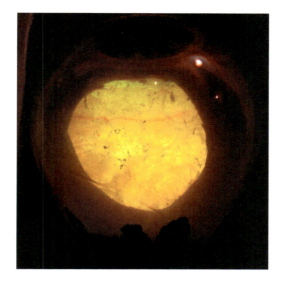 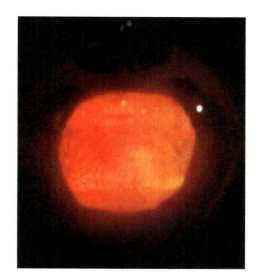

In the Apse amber and ruby glass
cast a warm glow as seven lamps
set alight the central niches.

No wicks or oil in the lamps,
bright or dark as Earth and time
and eye of the beholder.

Yellow glass has bubbles, veins,
like ancient resin's frozen life
we hang as jewels round our necks,

to remind us how our love is pulsed,
our blood's warm light glows amber, red
but sooner or later, darkened, dead.

The cool and sober day when shroud
veils hope, you know she won't return
despite the words you cry aloud.

Sarah knew how quickly love is lost,
(her church had arrows to attest)
carving pinecones, counting out her cost.

Her coloured glass repeats a tableau:
we refract light, warm it, pass it on;
via red and amber, find green light, go.

Stained Glass St Mary's, Wreay

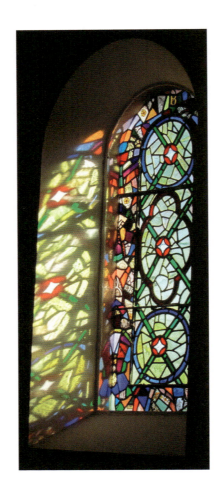

from
broken
fragments

re
assemble
light

stain
upon
white

lucencies

prismatic
sight

Nollekens' Monument to Lady Maria Howard 1789

Maria slumps, her body barely breathes,
her fingers still cover the lifeless hand
of her baby, whose small body splays
awkwardly from her right thigh, head hung down
on her lap; Maria is propped up
by a crouching female figure, sister
or angel, who urges her to look skywards.
Maria's neck has wilted, her eyes look on
the vacancy she feels; her left arm has dropped
away from her baby's head. Faint life ebbs,
she is the very type of grief unassuaged.

Sarah Losh and teenage sister Katharine
stand in the luminous Chapel and stare
at the shining marble figures before them.
They feel numb, such private anguish on display.
Henry Howard is their father's friend, now
remarried. The statue remains long after grief
has waned. If ever they should be parted,
they vow, none should come between; a statue
to their love will be warm in heart and mind,
not calculated marble.

1850 - Dunbar makes his final marks:
Sarah, aged 64, has three years left to live.
Katharine's statue, taken from sketches
Sarah made, shows a young woman in Naples,
bent over a pinecone, symbol of eternity.
Her love for Katharine will stay hidden
under tons of roughly carved sandstone,
a public private grief, the key to which
she alone has access,
she alone has reference.

Sarah's Arrow

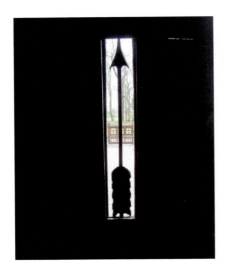 

'In the dark house of mortal dissolution'

Death and desire, desire and death…
the sharp point of an arrow,
its delicate feathers of flight,
rippling air to thump into wood,
stone or flesh – stuck in the church wall
on the left as you enter, stark and bare,
as if death leapt through the door,
fired a shaft, still quivering - a consummation,
in the small hours, you might have wished
in the dark days at Woodside
after Katharine died. Parted in life,
not yet united in death.

And poor William Thain, who sent a pinecone
from Afghanistan before he was killed,
the church nearing completion, did death
impale you again, how it would not let go
even as you carved symbols of resurrection?

With the oak doors closed,
narrow panes lowered
in the panels,
two iron arrows
puncture the light.

Apple Orchard, High Head Castle

Sun warmed terrace above the Ive,
an orchard seat, edenic apples
the reddest chromatics can muster;

so, for a time, time stops and wasps,
busy about the bruised and fallen,
suck and swallow silently;

a buzzard mews at a distance
and one could consider this calm
might stretch out, even to the end of time…

Clotted Air

The first snows of winter
settle on Northern Fells,
soften boundary wire
to patterned lattices.

Greenfinches scrabble nuts,
robins bluster, a chatter
of fieldfares strip the hawthorn,
flake after flake clots air.

November Snow

Afternoon flurries,
swept on the iced
wings of easterlies,
settle on fallen snow;

a weak sun lays
out warm feelers,
intensifies the light;

garden birds
peck anxiously
at peanuts and seeds;
a flock of lanced, long-tailed tits
fly in and feast,
their palest of pink breasts
fluffed out against the cold;

I fetch in more logs
and watch the feeding;
warm by the window,
I rest elbows on the solid table,
focus the field glasses
and feel my heart
beat
over and over,
sixty years

and counting.

Inscribed Lintel Franklin Cottage 1985

Step in, fill the sails, skim over waves,
feel timbers creak, taut cloth slapped with spray;
in the offing a dance of islands:
the edge of sight, the catch of salt air;

closer now, double summits puncture sky,
a dove claps overhead, a butterfly
winks with freshly painted, peacock wings;
we beach, raise our eyes to the hills;

see the long slope to Bowscale Tarn,
the sheer surrounds, the ladder climb,
Bannerdale, Foule Crag, Blencathra;
saddled there, a glimpse of spiralled tusk...

ridges etched with shadows, children
scramble Halls Fell, a black Labrador
wags ahead, laughter licks the wind;
this is home, enter engraved landscapes,
open the stamped and posted heart.

The new-made Path

curves from a garden gate,
lined with sea weathered bricks
of cream, rusticated reds
and assorted burnt clays
gathered from west coast Solway;
edged sandstone, mortared fast,
fragments of paua shell
glance pacific blues and greens,
limestone gravel banks off
towards the vegetables,
leaving a green island
of holly, fern, pheasant's eye.

Days of patient labour:
cement, point, find levels,
make good the half broken,
recycle old clay and shells,
adorn the curves in and out
of gates and passageways;
back and forth and back again,
tread and retread the path
that overbrims with rain
or radiates hot stone,
sometimes forgets itself
till impulse finds its feet
and we are off again

in step with what escaped us.

Castle Hewen

Most days I walk up here, past Midtown Farm,
up a steepish track, through a gate in the hedge
and left into a high field, overlooking fells,
woods, Eden valley and the Pennines beyond;
whatever the mood it is lightened and transfigured
with the wind lifting breath and shoulders,
views stitched together as you turn on your toes,
savouring each hairbreadth field of light and shade;

Scotland to the north, thin shouts of reivers skein upwards
with creel of curlew, skylark trance and mew of buzzard;
the debateable lands spliced by Hadrian's wall,
a pattern of field and wood, priory and Pele tower,
farm and steading. Solway Firth penetrates
the plain, sucking Esk and Eden, salinating
their lower reaches. Salmon weave upstream in Autumn,
leap rapids and weir, back to the birthing.

To the west Barrock Fell, the Roman road, Mosedale,
Blencathra's saddle, riding cloud bright hills to the sea.

To the south, buttercup yellow and saturated greens
of Eden, its woods and hedges, fields and drystone walls,
draining Mallerstang and the Ullswater valleys.

To the east, Cross Fell, its Helm winds, snow lingering
Pennine ways, the Fell-Edgers, Viking place names…

and back to where we started, vanished Castle Hewen,
Owain mab Urien's stonghold, its giant Caesarius
and drained Tarn Wadling, which cussedly
fills again in winter deluge – back to where we started,
the necessary perch, the overlooking.

Tree Sparrows Nesting – January 20th 2015

Winter sun, patchy snow, a stretch of light,
the feather in your beak finds nest space
as she watches from a hawthorn branch;
emerging, you join her, bill to bill,
cheek spots mingle, an excited 'tschip',
a blur of chestnut heads, of napes.

Several times through the threshold
then nothing for an hour – was it make
believe, before return to life and death
forage, the faint warmth of sun a feint
and nothing more, the beak-sharpening
mere practice, the 'tschip' a gesture of song?

But you're back again, chasing trespass,
energised, white cheeks flash fiercely;
one instinct sated, another lifts its head.

Back at my desk, desire in its keep,
I write a line, look out the window:
there is a space in everything,
the way that bright desire gets in.

Carlisle Cathedral

 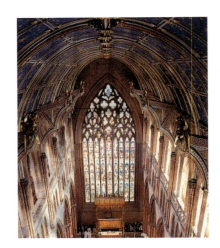

Dark must as you enter:
buckled Norman arches
crushed under tons of stone,
squat on stumped pillars.

Tower rears overhead,
dimly lit, dominant,
truncated nave splays
oppressive, imminent.

Turn right to the choir, from
Strickland's masterly stalls,
beast-hung misericords, double
take a vaulted roof of stars.

Backcloth lapis lazuli,
embossed in lustred gold,
hands that carved and lavished
paint, eight centuries cold.

Cathedral Face

Without a wrinkle, line or blemish,
without a working smile or tears,
your eyes are windows to a blankness,
unrevealing of your fears.

An angel or a woodman's wife,
staring down with huge dark eyes,
or Mary, who has gained a god
and lost a son she would have prized.

Sent Up

Step in, look up
through the atomic dust
of a million prayers,
the cumulative must
and breath of human earnest
pushed against
mullioned glass
and miles of air beyond.

Feel it, breathe in
an impulse of fellowship,
breathe out again
and watch the particles
of hope and loss
dissipate and settle
on sublimities of tracery,
blazed bright as blood
sunstruck through liquid glass
like the distant
implosion of a star.

Misericord 8 South side Carlisle Cathedral
'Woman about to beat a man'

Washing beetle raised in her right hand,
his beard grasped in her left,
mouth set, exultant.

He flinches away, hat disordered,
face pulled down by her fist
of beard, bested.

Carver's delight in the sexual battle,
women as viragos,
leading men to sin?

Or, simply, the dance of love,
first this way, then that, her thrust,
coupled with his, coupled back.

And the monk's bottom, resting above,
his hips sway with plain song,
his hands touch green oak.

Carlisle Castle Graffiti – making marks

To shape a stone,
carve a smooth boled beech with names
or paint rich ochred animals in caves,
to sign kaleidoscopic spray in alleyways
is part the same…

misericord, carved pews, desks,
graffitied stone or battlements,
hieroglyphics of loss or lust
signatures on blocks of marble…

we make our mark,
child, ditch or wall,
planted tree, ring or sword,
thumbprint, gravestone, painted hand,
foot in setting concrete,
carved bone, cornice, totem pole….

and here on dungeon walls
doomed prisoners carved with iron nails
a woman longed-for, desire and death
with arrowed wings, crosses, crowns,
things you carve because you can't express
how tomorrow's sweeter as you're losing life
with all its promises of spring,
each breath drawn, remembering.

Hadrian's Wall – Regina's Tombstone

'To the spirits of the departed and Regina, freedwoman and wife of Barates of Palmyra, a Catuvellaunian by race, thirty years old' (The Latin inscription)

'Regina, the freedwoman of Barates, alas' (The Palmyrene inscription)

Slave and 'queen' to Barates, who married you –
for how many years? You died aged thirty;
Your tribe's in South England, his in Syria,
the extremes of empire, two thousand miles apart.
Your fine tombstone at the end of Hadrian's wall,
his less fine, sixty miles west, where he died, aged sixty eight.

Your story, his, connection, separation,
hope in such disparate worlds – improbable
meeting, acculturation, love and death.

Look, your pose and dress, necklace, bracelets, wicker throne,
spindle and distaff, strongbox and baskets of wool,
a mix of Palmyrene and Roman art, coloured stone,
the tinctures of intercourse, age, gods and status.

Were you young, comely, he rich, older, acquisitive,
or of an age, his death years later, broken,
like his common stone? The stark Aramaic
'alas', slaps at the tongue, the shape of the word
like a boat full-rigged, sailing out of sight.

Scumbling in Grubbins Wood

Wet yews, black-boled, flesh wound red
jags through, visceral, livid;
viridian needles scratch trunkart,
oak and birch leaves, a pointillist
litter - ochres of dull russet,
distressed bronze, footprint pressed.

Scratch blue sky, branch printed -
through black frames of yew
tide recedes beneath crumbled
limestone; grey streak of heron
poses a static question mark,
clouds mass above Whitbarrow.

We lose track, double back,
find our way again: between
layers of yew, slivers of bright shore
torch shadows; we emerge
as the sun sinks baywards,
blazes the journey east.

Waverley Bridge

Abandoned sandstone bridge,
built on a curve of lost rails
over the river,
on the edge of the Vallum,
alongside the old canal,
heading north
to Edinburgh.

Crossroads,
cross Eden,
cross canal,
cross Hadrian's wall.

River meets bridge,
meets canal,
meets road,
meets wall.

Train, boat,
cart and beast
mingle with
the tramp of feet.

West coast road,
past mile forts,
Burgh by Sands,
Drumburgh castle,
to Bowness-on-Solway,
start of the Carlisle canal,
and west again
to the embankments,
girders of the Solway viaduct

and beyond
to Skinburness
and Maryport,
the end of the Hadrian's Wall,
over sealight to the Offing.

Sunset, the Military Road

Our road swoops and rises,
trailing the Wall, which heads East
high along Win Sill ridge.
Black shadows leak from tree and stone,
sheep elongate to cartoon horses,
dip into hedges of grass.

Loops of dark cloud drift towards us,
a far hill tranced in shafts of light;
lowering sun sears through screen,
eyes narrow to hold wheels steady
through switchback; surgical light
incises remnant Wall and Vallum.

Warm hands cut stone here, dug ditches,
laid foundations of fort and baths;
revealed again, entrenched, translated,
pace once more through imprints of wind;
two thousand years pause and pass,
bloodied clouds rear, fall and fade.

Solway Viaduct January 1881

Let me tell you about the dark,
half way across the viaduct,
midnight in the signal box,
floodwaters thick with ice forty feet below,
small ice floes on the receding tide
thumping against girders.

A clear stellar night,
we can see larger bergs
being dragged towards us
on our skeletal bridge
from the rivers at the Firth head:
collisions shake and rattle the girders…

Three a.m. – with a tremendous crash
one of the piers on the Bowness side collapses;
in the distance an iceberg approaches,
a hundred feet long and fifteen high;
it gleams in the star and icelight,
we hold our breath…

Two supports are swept aside,
twisted railshards topple down
in slow motion to the black water;
we start running, the four of us,
away from the signal box
towards the Scotch side,
the screech of ice and iron
splitting in our ears…

Next day at dawn,
a shocking sight:
the mile long viaduct twisted and torn,
a three hundred yard gap ripped through,
our box, its signal set at the all clear,
hangs by a thread.

Solway Offing

From Rockcliffe incline West,
beyond channel and marsh,
Edward's lonely monument,
shadows of the Roman wall,
derelict canal and viaduct.

Look out to the offing
where sunset-bloodied waters
scumble deeper into dusk.

Inland, a wetland centre
peers at waders, the distant
pyramid of Skiddaw solid,
cement-jacketed in winter snow.

Turn back to sea and scan;
there, in the distant paste
where sea meets sky, a sail,
another, and a third.

A gunwale linked with shields,
the splash of straining oars,
you turn your back to yell
but nothing's there, it's gone.

The empty offing stares,
for all your scalded search
the certain vision's passed,
backwatered, a drained cup
into Solway silence.

Skinburness - Peripheries of Sight

Caught by the slide of light,
a curved tilt of sea
floods the Offing with bright
edges of dark debris.

Now the break of day,
where thick light breeds
the blades of Solway
and Cumbria bleeds.

Sky Posts

Take the jetty, as it sinks
beneath water into sky,
causeway
to faint lucencies of cloud.

Posts anchored in air,
double up,
support deep
reflective blue.

Footsteps loosen ripples,
each one wobbles
water calming
sky

Threshold Light

Quiet step through the sprung wood:

dropped light patters on boughs,

curves to the red cliff – meadows

touched by the river vibrate

beyond the arc of shadows,

couple in the changeling light.

The End of Eden

Here at the outflow, a mile beyond Rockcliffe,
rain, which fell a hundred miles away,
issues into Solway. Time and distance
dissolve into a wider sea,
fresh water swallows wave on salty wave,
throws up on Burgh Marsh a brackish scum.

Glacial tarns, wells of the mountains,
release their milky becks, churned down
to feeder streams into Ullswater, Eamont,
join Eden, stutter North through Nunnery Gorge;
Hell Gill tumbles down Mallerstang, past Pele,
bastle, stone circle, tumuli, drystone walls.

Beaker people, Celt, Roman, Saxon, Norse,
bones mixed in blood red tilth fought over,
burnt, ravished by Reivers and soldiers
of both sides and those between; the river
washes all away, bone, sword, comb and grave,
branch and fallen bird, sluice to sea-bleached silence.

Eden and its tributaries
flush out ice age rocks and skeletal dreams,
still pastures, chapels bright with coloured glass,
barrel vaulted, collapsed ceilings, cracked bridges
crumple, arches breached in tree-stacked storms.

And each unfailing Spring, fresh April bursts, frail
snowdrops pierce frosted banks, bluebells brighten
under leafbirth beech, greenlight dapples everywhere.

The loving support of Irene, together with that of Will, Jonty and Bethan, has made possible the writing of these poems. Milly, our inspirational Labrador, has accompanied me on almost all of my excursions along the Eden. The poems are as much love poems to them all, as hymns of praise to this unparalleled valley.

I would like to thank Nick Jones for the use of his paintings on pages 6,7,16,24,25,28 and 30 and for his companionship on many fruitful walks alongside the Eden and its byways.

I would also like to thank Roger Pett for the use of his photographs on pages 34 and 45 and Kathryn Kimball for her photograph on page 73.

The photographs on pages 86 are from the Carlisle Cathedral website
www.carlislecathedral.org.uk

The photographs on page 91 are from judithweingarten.blogspot.co.uk

The drawing of the East Elevation of Armathwaite Castle is taken from page 196 of The Medieval Fortified Buildings of Cumbria by Denis Perriam and John Robinson, 1998.

For more information or comment please send an email to:
alandaltrey@gmail.com

Made in the USA
Charleston, SC
04 May 2016